Barbie through the Decades

DiscoverRoo
An Imprint of Pop!
popbooksonline.com

Barbie in the 1960s

by Elizabeth Andrews

WELCOME TO DiscoverRoo!

This book is filled with videos, puzzles, games, and more! Scan the QR codes* while you read, or visit the website below to make this book pop.

popbooksonline.com/sixties

abdobooks.com

Published by Pop!, a division of ABDO, PO Box 398166, Minneapolis, Minnesota 55439.

Printed in the United States of America, North Mankato, Minnesota.

052024
082024

THIS BOOK CONTAINS RECYCLED MATERIALS

Cover Photo: Getty Images

Interior Photos: Getty Images, Shutterstock Images, Wikimedia, Design Bay Productions, Associated Press, Alamy Stock Photo, MATTEL/SIPA/Newscom

Editor: Grace Hansen

Series Designer: Victoria Bates

Library of Congress Control Number: 2023947573

Publisher's Cataloging-in-Publication Data

Names: Andrews, Elizabeth, author.

Title: Barbie in the 1960s / by Elizabeth Andrews

Description: Minneapolis, Minnesota : Pop!, 2025 | Series: Barbie through the decades | Includes online resources and index

Identifiers: ISBN 9781098246259 (lib. bdg.) | ISBN 9781098246815 (ebook)

Subjects: LCSH: Barbie dolls--Juvenile literature. | Toys--History--Juvenile literature. | Nineteen sixties--Juvenile literature. | Toys--Social aspects--Juvenile literature. | Popular Culture--Juvenile literature.

Classification: DDC 688.722--dc23

*Scanning QR codes requires a web-enabled smart device with a QR code reader app and a camera.

TABLE OF Contents

CHAPTER 1

Barbie's Beginnings

Humans have made dolls for thousands of years. At first, dolls were made of clay, straw, or other natural materials. As the world changed, so did dolls. The toys got more detailed and exciting. In 1959, the fashion doll, Barbie, hit store shelves. The doll game was never the same.

WATCH A VIDEO HERE!

Barbie's original striped swimsuit was inspired by fashions worn in the 1950s.

Ruth Handler was the creator of Barbie. Ruth and her husband owned the toy company Mattel Creations. Ruth noticed that children's dolls were mostly baby dolls. She believed growing girls didn't want to play with babies. They wanted dolls that encouraged them to dream of their futures.

Ruth Handler was born in Denver, Colorado, in 1916.

Mattel released the first Barbie in 1959. She wore a black-and-white swimsuit, black high heels, white sunglasses, and gold earrings. Barbie was a teenage fashion model from Willows, Wisconsin. She cost $3. Her extra outfits ranged between $1 and $5.

The Handler family

DID YOU KNOW?

Barbie's full name is Barbara Millicent Roberts. She was named after Ruth's daughter Barbara.

The first Barbie commercial played during an episode of The Mickey Mouse Club.

Barbie was a hit! In the first year, Mattel sold 350,000 dolls. Soon customers were asking for more. Mattel went on to create friends, dreamhouses, cars, and more than 250 careers for Barbie. Ruth was right. Children did like grown-up dolls. Their imaginations grew with Barbie!

The first Barbie appeared passive and gentle. She fit into the late 1950s female tradition of **homemaking** and beauty **trends**. Some of the first Barbies included Barbie Learns to Cook and Suburban Shopper Barbie. However, Ruth wouldn't keep Barbie in the home for long.

Suburban Shopper Barbie, 1959

CHAPTER 2

Living in the Real World

Beyond Barbie, the 1960s was an important decade, especially in America. The country went through big **cultural** changes. Because Mattel is based in the United States, newly-released Barbies often connected with **current affairs** and movements in the US.

LEARN MORE HERE!

The mini skirt was a symbol of changing female roles.

First Lady Jacqueline Kennedy was very popular with women and girls. Her style inspired many of Barbie's early 1960s looks.

President John F. Kennedy was elected in 1960. The US was in a time period known as the Cold War. For years, Soviet-controlled countries and the US competed to be the best in many areas including technology.

In 1964, the US military began requiring men to fight in Vietnam. Some Americans

DID YOU KNOW? Counterculture was a social movement encouraging peace, love, equality, and change.

did not support the war in Vietnam. Their dislike led to the counterculture movement. This movement included feminists who wanted equality for women. Many women in the '60s were tired of their required role as **homemakers**.

Large groups of young people came together to protest the Vietnam War.

FREEDOM
WE DEMAND
EQUAL RIGHTS NOW!
WE DEMAND
AN END TO POLICE BRUTALITY NOW!
WE MARCH FOR
INTEGRATED SCHOOLS NOW
WE MARCH FOR
FIRST CLASS CITIZENSHIP NOW!
WE MARCH FOR
EFFECTIVE CIVIL RIGHTS LAWS NOW

One of the most important movements during the 1960s was the Civil Rights Movement. Black Americans were treated unfairly. **Jim Crow laws** were still being used in the South. Civil rights leaders worked to pass laws that helped Black Americans and all people receive fair treatment. It was an empowering time for Black Americans.

In the 1960s, Black and white students didn't go to the same schools. Schools for Black students were often in poor condition.

CHAPTER 3

Sixties Barbie Fashion

The first decade of Barbie brought more characters to the Barbie Universe (BU). Mattel released Barbie's boyfriend Ken in 1961. Children could pick the blonde or brunette version of Ken. Barbie's first friend, Midge, was released in 1963. She had freckles and short hair.

EXPLORE LINKS HERE!

Ken's friend Allan was released in 1964.

DID YOU KNOW?

Ken was named after the Handlers' son Kenneth.

The 1960s brought new faces, hairstyles, and clothing for Barbie. Barbie's eyes, though still not looking straight ahead, were more open and less downcast. Barbie's cheeks got fuller, and her eyebrows became less arched. Bubblecut Barbie was very popular. Her hair came in many colors.

Fashion Queen Barbie, released in 1963, came with three hairstyles.

Most Barbies were sold wearing swimsuits. It encouraged people to buy more clothes.

During the early 1960s, Barbie's clothes were very girly. She often wore full skirts with defined waists. In 1964, Swirl Ponytail Barbie was released. She came in a red swimsuit. Children often dressed her in nicely-**tailored** clothes.

Later in the 1960s, fashions changed in the real world. Mod was the newest **trend** taking hold, and young people were leading the way. Barbie got a mod makeover too. Her hair got longer. Her clothes had a more relaxed fit and were made in brighter colors.

Poodle Parade Barbie, 1965

A new version of Barbie's body came out in 1967. It was called Twist 'N Turn Barbie. Barbie's legs bent so children could pose her in new ways. Barbie's friends had the new body as well. Talking Barbie came out in 1968. She said things such as, "Would you like to go shopping?" and "I have a date tonight."

A 1960s advertisement showing Barbie's ability to bend her legs.

CHAPTER 4

Big Steps for Barbie

Ruth Handler wanted girls to dream about their futures when they played with Barbie. Registered Nurse Barbie came out in 1961. Nursing was Barbie's first career. The doll came with glasses, a hot water bottle, and a diploma!

COMPLETE AN ACTIVITY HERE!

Nursing was and has been a career dominated by women. The job focuses on giving medical care to others.

Miss Astronaut Barbie and Mr. Astronaut Ken each came with an American flag.

NASA sent astronauts into space throughout the 1960s. The US was competing with the Soviets over who could get to the moon first. In 1965, Miss Astronaut Barbie and Mr. Astronaut Ken were released. Mattel used the excitement of space exploration to help kids reach for the stars!

Barbie Dreamhouse

In the 1960s, the feminist movement encouraged girls to think about their futures outside the family home. In 1962, the first ever Barbie Dreamhouse was released. It was a single-room home with stylish sixties decor, a stereo, and college flags. At the time, only 0.1 percent of women owned their own home.

Ruth knew the world was changing in the 1960s. The Civil Rights Movement boosted powerful Black voices. Mattel believed that Black children deserved to see themselves in the dolls they played with.

Christie (center) and other Barbie dolls wore mod styles. Their clothing was bright and had bold patterns.

Black Francie did not get her own special mold. She had the same features as white Barbie dolls.

In 1968, Mattel released Talking Christie, the first Black doll created for the BU. Christie was Barbie's friend. She was made from her own special **mold**. She had a short mod hairstyle and wore a swimsuit. Christie was a huge success!

DID YOU KNOW?

In 1967, Mattel released a darker-skinned version of Barbie's friend Francie.

Julia

Julia was one of the first celebrity Barbie dolls. She was modeled after Diahann Carroll and released in 1969.

Julia was a popular **sitcom** about a mother. After her husband died in the Vietnam War, Julia was left to raise her son and work as a nurse. Diahann Carroll played Julia on the show. Carroll won a Golden Globe for best actress after the first season.

The 1960s were just the beginning for Barbie! Children loved Barbie and all her friends. Toy creators at Mattel had their own big dreams for the next chapter in the Barbie Universe!

A music record called Barbie Sings *features six jazz songs performed by Barbie and Ken.*

Making Connections

TEXT-TO-SELF

Have you ever played with Barbie or her friends? If so, what kind of life did you imagine for them? If not, what kind of life would you imagine?

TEXT-TO-TEXT

Have you read any books about other toys? What did those toys have in common with Barbie? How were they different?

TEXT-TO-WORLD

The Civil Rights Movement inspired Mattel to release Christie, the first specially-designed Black friend of Barbie. With the help of an adult, research other ways the Civil Rights Movement changed the world. Write a few sentences about what you found most interesting.

Glossary

cultural — of or relating to culture. Culture is the customs, arts, and ideas of a nation or people at a certain time.

current affairs — important events that are happening in the world.

homemaking — the job of caring for a household by cooking, cleaning, and raising children. A person who does this is a homemaker.

Jim Crow Laws — laws that forced separation between white people and Black people in public spaces.

mold — an unfilled space in which an object is shaped.

sitcom — a television show that involves a continuing cast of characters in a series of funny circumstances.

tailored — styled with nice straight lines and fit perfectly to the wearer.

trend — a current style or preference especially concerning clothing.

Index